Illusions and Freedom

SHOUNAK SARKAR

Beauty is eternity gazing at itself in a mirror

But you are eternity and you are the mirror

-    *Khalil Gibran*

Palace of Illusion and Freedom

I tiptoe to the door of the Palace
The kingdom where illusions float free
I open the lock with my mind's eye
I take a deep breath and step in to be free

The air in the Palace lulls me
It takes me in for a treat
I soon find myself floating with the angels
The earth looks like a mindless concrete

The girl in the cafe beckons me from below
She smells of Nescafe
However tempting it is to go down and have
a sip
Freedom is not the price to pay

I see my friends playing soccer
Their feet are tired and frayed
They ask me to join their nostalgic past
I fly by, picking samosas from their tray

I roam through sunsets and dahlias
Harmonies and musical valleys
I roam through purple abir
Apsaras and drunken alleys

The sun clock reminds me I need to return
To ground myself in boredom
But how do I turn back in a palace with no
roads
The Palace of Illusion and Freedom

****

Visions

I was born with a poor sight
What I couldn't see I couldn't decide
I grasped any straw that floated by
I swam upstream and I survived
And I learnt the art of a good fight

Then god blessed me with a different gift
That allowed me to see things in fourths
and fifths
I no longer require my eyes to behold
Visions of souls or dreams of gold
My mind can sense the ancient hieroglyphs

I can hear love from those that I rarely
see
I can feel the need from just the voice
I can sense elegance and grace in emptiness
I can float and touch the stars
I now have a vision limitless and free

My mind travels where my eyes missed the
lead
My senses follow the search
My body dances to the melody I hear

My soul soaks every moment received
Love is not left alone to bleed

****

Miss Bucephalus

She stands in front of her shadow
Head hung with desire and shame
She wants to step in the darkness
She wants to experience the game
She wants to do what others do
She wants to be untamed

But she is afraid of her own profile
Too timid to step on her own make
So she summons Alexander
To put a bridle on her neck
To turn her towards the sun
So she can get her own break

Did she really need Alexander?
Did she really need to be told?
Or was it just an excuse
A pretense for her to be bold
She could have galloped towards the sun
She didn't have to be sold!

She may not have had amassed the riches
She may not have had her picture on the
wall

She would just have been Miss Bucephalus
Just another mare
A mare unafraid of her shadow
A lady not afraid to fall.

****

The Day After

She was a Cinderella waiting to happen
A white rose tied in plastic and strings
Sheltered from birth
Nurtured by her family and kin
Allowing her to bloom and be seen

Her slippers were always tied firmly to her
feet
Her dainty hands cuffed with her wedding
bands
Her face always dazzling and demure
Never precocious or bold
An order she followed as told

Years went by.....
While her eyes still lured a hundred suitors
And her hands still felt like silken muslin
Her shoes showed the wrinkles
Her cuffs turned brittle Her dress felt
cold
The petals were still soft but the wrappers
were old

Then, one fine evening....

She broke her chains and dropped her veil
Took one slipper and left it like a precious
grail
To the Midnight Ball she whispered to her
friends
One foot firmly on her solitary shoe, the
other foot making amends

I still remember the ball...
Cinderella danced like never before
Like the many Prince Charmings
I searched in vain for the slipper or the
soul

It was hard the day after, even for the
saints
For mere mortals, were we ever in the game
To hold Cinderella's slippers
Not just for the night
Not just for the fast lane.
So, I did what I always do, I let the night
just float by in vain

****

Dance Of Your Life

You came to the floor to dance with your
life
And tripped on your high-heeled shoes
You asked your partner for a hand
But he was preoccupied with his own blues

You looked around for a handsome man
Who could lift you back to your feet
But they were all swaying with their lovers
Toe to toe, cheek to cheek

Your eyes paused for a fleeting moment
On the Devil, dressed in vain
But you are too pious to take that path
Enjoy the pleasure with the pain

With nowhere to go, you knelt on the floor
And prayed to the Almighty
He answered "Look at you
You are your own deity"

You then asked your soul again and again
To help you with your heels

Soul whispered "It is simple dear, take
them off
Dance....and see how it feels"

****

A Short Story

A short story, if written well
Leaves the reader wanting more
Chekov, Hemmingway, Gogol, Maupassant
They enter your mind but never go

A short story is what we open
When seeking for comfort nonexistent
In no time you are in a plot
That is familiar yet comfortably distant

A short story is the source
Of plays and movies galore
A podcast? An essay?
The writer is not needed anymore

But a short story is always unfinished
Like the tea at the bottom of the cup
We savor, we sip, we smell the words
But wonder how the end is so abrupt

Fear of the Night

It is cold, the night is dreary
I stand naked and weary
Searching for those faces in the dark
The smiles that were always warm
The touch that helped my calm
Have they left me in the park?

The lover enjoys the evening but seeks the
night
The loner likes the solitude but waits for
the day to light
Who am I kidding, I just feel shitty tonight

No smile, no touch, no loving hand
The cold wind takes all it can
I cling to what I have
A cup of tea or a glass in hand

A Selfish Journeyman

[In memory of my mother and her fight with
Alzheimer's]

It comes into the world fearless and fragile
Protected by the very body it owns
It grows unseen, like the Dutchman's Pipe
Till it takes over her name, her fame, her
soul.

It is restless as time goes on
Unquenchable in its pursuit
Seeking every pleasure, dreaming every
dream
Her happiness the laughter in the crowd
Her vanity the swish of her Gucci on her
skin
Her sadness the cries over her unforgiven
lover
An empress, floating through the hallways
of gilded sun beams

It doesn't know to slow down or to stop
Catching every note, every thought
Till its wings are too heavy to fly
And suddenly it can but only walk

"How can that be", it rages
"Who do I turn to", it thinks
There are no answers silly
No eternal gilded sunbeams

It stumbles through the darkness
Dragging her along
Tripping over every stone
Her body the bearer of its fractured form
Selfish as always it decides to leave
Closing the shutters, locking the doors
Nobody can see what it left behind
Protected as always, by the body it owes

While there she lies
A shriveled reminder of her wholesome
past
It leaves her when she needed it most
Stripping her of her dignity, oblivious to
her pain
A selfish journeyman who doesn't look back
Are you truly the one bereft of any soul?

Aging

Do I always need a muse?
What drives me to seek boredom?
What happened to the restlessness?
My son calls it aging. Happened in the
summer of 2017 he says.

When did I turn to swirling the wine?
When did sleep become important?
When did large gatherings become
annoying?
My son calls it aging. Happened in the
summer of 2017 he says.

The baritone voice of Cohen
Nina's air fried kababs with Patagonian
Malbec
The tranquil view of the ever changing
ocean from the Royal Coast Condo
Flipping through old albums
I call that aging. Happens every tomorrow
I say

Amabashya

It was a moonless summer night
I sat on a bench by the sea
A warm wetness lapped my ankles
It was just the waves, the sand and me

Then I saw the shadowy sketch out far
Gracefully riding the waves
It was there and it was not
Who was it out there, so tiny but so brave

The shadowy sketch stood on a silver surf
And started hurtling towards me
I sat frozen in time and space
Numb, petrified yet excited and somehow
free

The silver surf crashed on the beach
As the contour crashed on my lap
I closed my eyes and opened my arms
As it covered me like a silken wrap

I found myself in the Garden of Eden
An apple in my mouth

Was this that sinful I wonder
To experience the night without guilt or
doubt

****

DA-97

She is oil, he is water
She floats, for him it is all about matter
She sparks her shine and color
He would rather be the essence below her
She rides his waves
He holds her above
Till they come to the shore where he dumps
her

She is the lamp which lights the room
He the switch behind the door
She creates the mood bright or night
Glows in others appreciation and delight
He is unknown, unseen, told to remain so
Till he decides to flick off and leave her in
her incandescent glow

She is the voice, he the beat
Mothers hum her tunes, others tap their
feet
Her face is there on every wall
His hand and sticks a forgotten cast
Till the drumming stops
The voice sounds lonely,

Searching for the rhythm that was
supposed to last

****

Good Morning

Wake up dear, the tea is ready
Let your dreams swirl and float
Put on your slippers, wrap your scarf
Get into your same old coat

The nite is gone and so is the Prince
Morning beckons you to your daily chores
The kid needs his breakfast, the car needs
a wash
Hubby needs his kiss, the dog is waiting at
the door

You can sip the first sips
And savor your dreams of last night
It is hot, earthy, burns your lips
A bliss that was a journey of delight

Open the apps, there is news from abroad
Scroll your fingers over the screen
Lost amongst weddings and bank frauds
Is there a note from Prince Charming?

Look yourself in the mirror

Pause and bring on your inner smile
It is just another day, my dear
The night is round the corner, just wait
awhile

****

Hollow Night

When the night is hollow
Do the waves still roll on the sand
Do the crickets sing louder
Does the bottle look empty in a hand

Do the fingers itch for a half smoked joint
Do dreams recede behind the cloud
Does the brain stumble and stutter
Does the Devil always seem loud

Request a small intermission
From this cruel state
Night, you seduce and you lure
But you serve the dish too cold too late

Snapshots

There is a portrait in my palm
An artist's rendition of innocence and
grace
A stroke of the brush over sensuous copper
A smile that shows her heart a trace
Her necklace in ruby and gold
Adorning her neck, her husband's pride
As her eyes look up and say to the world
I am not just a beautiful bride

There is a reel stored in the recesses of
my brain
A directors capture of freedom and joy
A close shot of a face unwashed and
uncombed
A runaway look, both darting and coy
One hand hug a coffee mug, the other on
the wheel
A yellow dress, falling off one shoulder
Eyes squinted to hold her smile that
declares
I am just newer and bolder

The Soldier

Numbed by the touch that he never feels
Blinded by the light he never sees
Dimmed by the sound that he never hears
He is a soldier, impenetrable in his deep
freeze.

He knows that there is a lady faraway
Whose touch can be the balm
Whose words can be the music
Whose smile can be the charm

Yet he puts on his armor at the break of
dawn
Ensures his senses don't long for those
that don't belong
He steadies his hand, steels his gut
Peers through his rifle scope
At the icy veneer of his calloused heart

But as one more day passes in the trenches
of aimless fight
As the sun gives way to the lunacy of
heavenly moonlight

The soldier leaves his trenches and strips
off every tights
He opens his soul to the lady's delight

The grass embalms him with her feathery
touch
The wind plays him her honeyed songs
The stars charm him with their thousand
smiles
He is a lover, if only for tonight

****

Lullaby

She wanders in her own fears
The faceless names, the constant calls
from the darkest abyss of her mind
Clinging to those dearest - it is their touch,
their tone, their feel that still lingers in
her brain.

A withering flower, left alone.
The stale smell reminds us of her morning
fragrance
Her beauty, her grace, her love.
She blossomed in those early morn
Weathered the scorching heat as the sun
traveled its arc
But fell from her tree, unmoored, before
darkness fell.

A child with no future
A child with a past that seen through the
frosty mirror of her own mind
Seems dark, frightening, haunting.

She needs her sleep, her peace, her rest
She is a child of age but a child no less

She needs her lullaby
A lullaby of old age

****

Self Absorbed

I thought and thought again
If I etch a small tattoo, will that be in vain
Will it be an anchor over the shoulder
Or should I place it in some place bolder
May be it should just be in my brain
Or carry it in my chest. A daisy chain.

I thought and thought again
If I click my selfie, will that be insane
Will I do it in my best attire
Or in my bath with nothing but desire
May be it should be just a click of the mind
A capture that doesn't stay still. Not
confined.

I thought and thought again
I etched my tattoo, I made it my friend
I snapped my selfie, here and there
I said to myself, I don't care
I like my body, I like my skin
What is already in my heart is not going to
dim
I need the magic, I need the balm
Nothing stops from sharing my charm

Ten Feet Away

Ten feet across she sits
Her hair hastily knotted, eyes fresh from
sleep
Busy with her plans for the day
Chiding her husband away
The lantern waits to be lit

She frisks between the kitchen and her
seat
The dinner done, the beds made
Takes her time with her dress
Her kurta ironed to be in shape
The lantern waits to be lit

Night falls, darkness descends
She takes her bath, plaits her beads
Pours the oil and lights the fuse
The lantern glows and lights the room
She looks up and sees
Ten feet away, the shadow recedes

Kolkata Summer

It is a wet dawn
The sun struggles to wake from his slumber
The cars gently go by, splashing the freshly
made puddles
The heavy smell of rain still hangs on the
window sills
The sparrow chirps for its daily rice.
Are you awake, my dear.

It is a hazy afternoon
The April sun scorches the city
The traffic has picked up Cars chasing
down the street in infinite sequence
The black asphalt parched, cracked, beaten
lifeless
The sweat gently pushing from every pore
Too lazy to roll down.
Are you dreaming, my dear

It is a sweltering night
The heat descends from the ceiling
Heavy, oppressive, unforgiving
Mosquitoes, hazy neon lights
TV screen the only respite

The body gives in, accepting defeat.
Are you sleeping, my dear

****

Starbucks

The black tress
The yellow dress
The Ajanta eyes
The smiling smiles
Rings in every finger
Warding off evil harbingers?
Corporate watch, earthy and bold
The bracelet dazzling gold
Voice of honey and steel
Tasking menials, making deals
Coffee and cake, take a break
It is Friday evening, for heaven's sake

Morning Slumber

The night is just over, the bed still a mess
My eyes are still closed, head foggy at best
Smell of tea wafts in and out of my dreams
I hear your footsteps, like a cat on
concrete beams
What is your hurry? Where do you need to
go?

I want you back beside me, I want to hold
I want to feel the soft butter, that is
never cold
The smell of abandoned love is still to early
to forsake
I know you are washing away your last
night's make
What is your hurry? When do you need to
go?

Is it just your habit to wake up with the
sun
Or is it the office that makes you leave the
fun
Do you have another family, another one to
see

Is it only when it is dark that you search
for me
If I was Muddy, if I could crow
I would sing " Baby, Please don't go"

****

Summer Breeze

I feel the summer breeze coming
I feel it at my door
It sways my restless mind
It lifts me off my floor

It smells of lilac and dewdrops
It mingles with my sweat
It caresses every part of me
I forget my frown and my fret

People say, "Don't open the door
The wind is a killer sublime
It puts you in a state of passion
The storm that follows kills you in a dime"

I say "I will open the door
I will smell and feel the breeze
I will face the thunder when it roars
I will take the storm till it cease"

I will then close my open shutters
And draw my curtains close
My summer breeze will be with me
Warm, honeyed, it will whisper as it blows

Ma

Ma, do you ever wonder why you can't
sleep?
Why doesn't your son come by every day?
Why does Baba never leave the house?
Or, is it all about rearranging the half torn
cotton strip over and over again?

Ma, do you listen to the daily orders telling
you what not to do?
The songs wafting from the red Saregama
Carvaan
The TV pundits analyzing the war on
Ukraine?
Or, is it just the inner voices that surround
you?

Do you feel the love of your daughter?
Do you feel taken care of by all?
Do you feel proud of your progeny?
Or, do you feel just abandoned and lonely?

We will never know Ma
All we know is that we took you for granted.
There was always food on the table

There was always the caring when one fell
sick
We never saw your pain, your sacrifice,
your suffering
So it is ok if today you don't see ours

****

The Kiss

It is sweet, it is soft
It sucks your lips like a honey dipped cloth
It tears up your face with its abandoned
joy
It is the kiss from your baby boy
You take it and love him...forever

It is a peck, it is a graze
It touches you softly and
leaves you unfazed
It is gentle, sometimes sad
It is the kiss from your Mom and Dad
You carry it in our heart ...wherever

It is rough and beaten
You are still horribly smitten
It scars your perfect lips
You pocket the bloodied kerchief for your
keeps
It is the kiss you always wanted
No you say....never

The Dove and the Falcon

You there white pigeon
Why do you perch on my bedroom sill
The tilt of your neck
The baby coos
You want to come in, I feel.

Everytime I open the window
Why do you flutter away
The darting eyes
The silken feathers
I know you want me to say 'Please Stay'

I know you know my bedroom
I know you watch my every move
Nestling close
Sweet nothings
Y're there as long as no one knows it is you.

Forgive me dove I don't want your peace
I want something new and strange
The unknown stranger
The beast
The one who will make me deranged

You there white falcon

Why do circle so high and above
Piercing eyes
Steel talons
Are you setting your eyes on the dove

You swoop, she faints
You pluck her away tucked in your frame
Another day
Another dove
But you never stopped to hear my refrain

Everytime I open the window
I just hear your screech
Those eyes
Those feathers
Why are you beyond my reach

I know you know my bedroom
I know you watch my every move
Fly high
Be pretentious, cavalier
But take me with your swoop

Desire

There is a place between the nose and the
cheeks
Below the bones, above those lips
That I want

There is an eyelid behind the falling
tresses
Beside the laughing left eye, hidden to
dazzle your graces
That I want

There is the crease in the contours of the
neck
Saying find me as it nestles in your blue
make
That I want

Lake

As the mist rises from the lake
Like a blanket slowly lifted from the lover
deep in her morning slumber
So does my mind swirl upwards
and reaches for the skies above
Too selfish to wait for anybody
Too ephemeral to care or to love

Two At a Time

Two days before I catch the plane
Two hours tonight before I wake up again
Oh, When can I break these invisible chain
Of time, one that shackle my body and my
brain

Two years gone since I saw the sea
Two decades since Haley passed by me
Oh, How many twos remains to be counted
Before the clock stops and I dare to chase
her, undaunted
Shall I wait for fate to find my future
Or let the future be unchained by me

Why

We want to swim with the fishes
We want to soar with the birds
But why is it when we walk with people
We feel lonely and apart?

We want our good friends around us
We love to drink and to dine
But why do we seek the cracks in the
windows
Through which to fly and fly

We want to sleep in our Caspers
We want our Memory foams
But then why when we go to bed
We keep fiddling with our phone

Come Over

Come over dearest
Come close to me
Come, cross the ocean
Come over, break free

Don't think about tomorrow
Just come over now
Don't think about nothing
Past promises, past vows

Is it those phrases that sweetens my
mouth
Is it those sounds that I want to hear
Or, is it the possibility that you'll never
come
That I always fear

The Veil

If the veil is green
It is there to conceal
The smile, the twinkle
The tears, the feel

If the veil is red
It is there to seduce
The hungry eyes
Of those who look

If the veil is black
If the veil is white
They are just symbols
Of what is wrong or right

But why do you have a veil that has no
color?
Are you hiding or do you want to share?
I think I know now, I am not spooked
It is the looking glass that you want
yourself to look

Surrender

You can put me on your head
I will be your crown
You can leave me as I am
I will not frown
You can embed me in your pearly necklace
I will shine
You can barter me for anyone else
I will be fine
You can hug me tightly in your bosom
I will snuggle
You can tie me to your loneliness
I will not struggle
What do you want to do with me
It is up to you ma'am
It is me after all
I am who I am

Sleep

Oh sleep! You fragile child
They plunder you from every side
From the midnight texts that sear your
brain
To yesteryears' ugly memories
From the cruelest words shared in office
To the wistful sounds of the future

All you need is a warm bed
A soft touch of assurance
Sweet whispers that float into you
Not the past, nor the future
But the comforting dark your fall into

The Moment

It is not about the future
It is not about the past
It is about the moment
The one that always last

Addiction

I need it when I awake
I want it before I go to sleep
The hollow passages in my hallway
Needs the heavy ambrosia, the refill

I stare aimlessly at the TV
Fidgety, restless, I twitch
Why can't I ignore it
The sweet nothings, the itch

Give me back my freedom
I scold my lazy brain
Take me away from this witch
You don't like it, it replies
You hypocritical bitch

It is just a smoke, it wafts, it drifts
It floats into the inner recesses of my guilt
It eats away at the very existence
The one I have so carefully built

But it is the one I wait for twice a day
Twice a day to keep
Once in the morning
And one before I go to sleep

The Ancient Fort

The king built his fort on the oceanfront
Impregnable, dark and foreboding
Years passed and the walls showed cracks
The ocean swirled, all knowing
And the water flowed in

The king was weary, war beaten and tired
Mused and wondered what to do
Unknowing to him light also poured in
And a garden grew

The Child in the Toy Shop

The child runs to the toy shop
Her face, a mess of breathless dews
Her toy has arrived
She has seen it from the street
It is there for her to keep

"Sir!, I want that doll", she cries
"It is sold", the keeper replies
"No,ooo", she wails
"It is mine"
"What a spoilt brat", the keeper pines

The toys stares from high on the shelf
"I can't speak, but I have a say"
"I have a heart, a mind"
It winks
The child never blinks

"It is mine I know"
"My dreams said so", says the child
"Whew", the owner has to say
While the toy mutters
"My face is a mess of breathless dews"

She Tried

She looks at the mountains
She looks at the sky
"Luv You", she says
To them that meets her eyes

The breeze takes the message
To the mountains and the sky
They answer not
"Oh, come on!", she says, "At least, try"

They hear me not, she thinks
She packs her bags and jumps on the engine
with wings
"Luv You", she whispers
To them that meets her eyes

The cloud takes the message
To the mountains and the sky
They answer not
"Oh, come on!", she says, "At least, try"

She is back on earth, she steps off the
plane
I am home, she declares to the faces with
no names

"Luv You", she whispers
To them that meets her eyes

The cloud takes the message
To the mountains and the sky
They answer
"You are home, we know. You tried"

****

Candles Burning in the Rain

[First reunion of Indian Students at Rice]

We came from places faraway
We were so young, so vain
Engineers, scientists or just wanderers
We were all in the same train

We glowed in our own reflection
We sipped beer in the dark
We danced on the beaches of Galveston
We played music in the car park

Few scores have gone by since
The fire may just now be a glow
Some just moved miles away
Some just left forever our shore

It doesn't matter wherever we are
The memories etched in our brain
Still shine brightly around us
Like candles burning in the rain

When The Ink Runs Dry

The pen is stuck, the ink dries
The pages turn over like a lover unsatisfied
The story is unfinished, left behind
Was it meant to be this unkind

Will it be a new pen that will spark the
scribble
Or is it just the ink that requires to dribble
May be it is the paper that will reignite the
fire
Stories must finish to one's desire

May be it is time to take a break
To look at same things with a new take
May be we don't need the paper, the pen,
the ink
All we need is a heart that beats and a mind
that can think